DATE DUE

DEC 3 1986			
OCT. 20 1987			
DEC. 1 5 1988			
MAY 1 7 1989			
NOV. 2 3 1989			
NOV. 0 7 1994			
MAR 1 9 1997			
JAN. 1 5 1000			
MAR 0 6 1003			
SEP 1 7 2003			
FEB 0 7 2005			
MAR 0 7 2005			
NOV 2 1 2006			
APR 2 7 2007			
DEC 1 7 2007			

HIGHSMITH 45-220

A robot arm seen performing its full range of movements.

Designer   Cooper-West
Editor   James McCarter
Art Director Charles Matheson
Researcher Dee Robinson
Consultant Tony Search
Illustrator Steve Braund

© Aladdin Books Ltd

Designed and produced by
Aladdin Books Ltd
70 Old Compton Street
London W1

First Published in the
United States in 1984 by
Franklin Watts
387 Park Avenue South
New York, NY 10016

ISBN 0-531-04816-0

Library of Congress No 84-50614

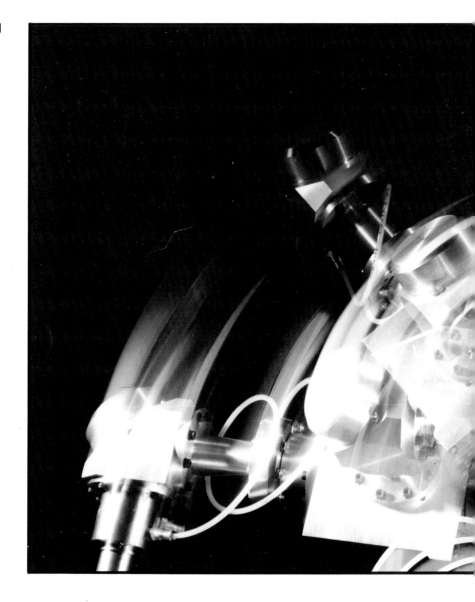

The Electronic Revolution

ROBOTS
AND COMPUTERS

Nigel Hawkes

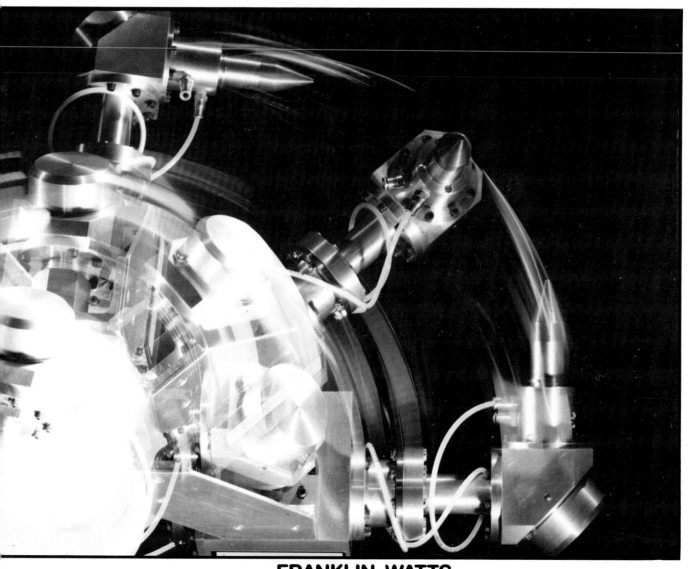

FRANKLIN WATTS
New York·London·Toronto·Sydney

Foreword

If you saw a typical robot you might not be too impressed. It would probably be a mechanical arm with a tool such as a paint-sprayer attached at the end – not at all like the "tin men" of science fiction films.

Real robots are simply tools that do our work for us, or make our work easier. People have been using similar machines ever since the first factories were built. The big difference with robots is that they work under computer control. As this book shows, robots are being used in many different areas of today's world. With computers becoming increasingly powerful, the robots of the future are sure to play an exciting part in our lives.

TONY SEARCH: *Technical consultant*

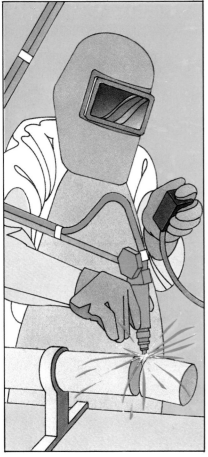

Lasers

Computers

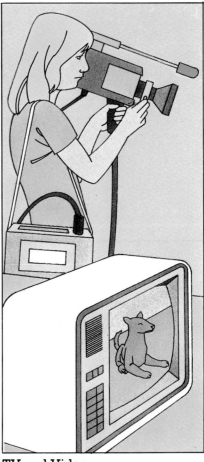

TV and Video

Contents

Radio and Radar

Satellites

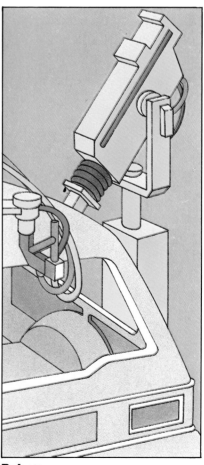

Robots

What is a robot?

A robot is a machine designed to imitate certain human actions. It need not look at all like a human being, but it must perform its tasks automatically. The word "robot" was first used by the Czech playwright Karel Capec in 1920, in a play he called *Rossum's Universal Robots*. Rossum designed and built an army of industrial robots which eventually became too clever and took over the world. Capec chose the word "robot" from the Czech word *robota*, which means "forced work." His vision of robots ruling people has since been the subject of many science fiction books and films.

Robot workers

Today we may not worry much about robots taking over people's lives. But we do worry about them taking over people's jobs. Robots can work 24 hours a day, without rest or coffee breaks, and for many routine jobs they are more reliable than human beings. On the other hand, robots free people from boring, repetitive work.

▽ Ordinary traffic lights are simple machines that operate on a set timetable. But if they are connected by computers to automatic sensors in the road that count the cars passing and then adjust the switching of the lights accordingly, they are robots.

△ There are many "robot" toys. This robot arm is not really a robot — it only operates under direct human control.

▷ Bigtrak has a small computer "brain." Its movements are programmed by pressing buttons on a simple keyboard. The very simplest robots work in a similar way.

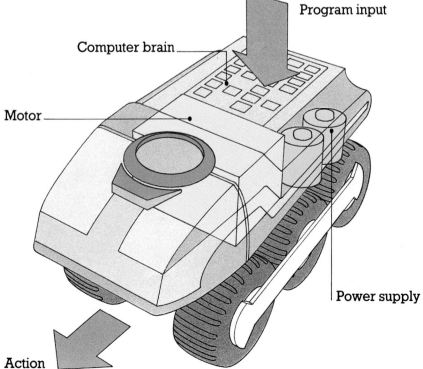

Program input

Computer brain

Motor

Power supply

Action

9

Science-fiction robots

Science fiction robots are nothing new. In Homer's epic poem, *The Iliad*, one of the first stories ever written, mechanical girls made of gold helped Hephaestus, a god who was also a blacksmith. In the 18th and 19th centuries, many ingenious automatic dolls were made, often powered by clockwork. Perhaps the most famous robots of all are C3-P0 and R2-D2, the mechanical heroes of the *Star Wars* films. Robots like C3-P0, which look like people, are called androids.

▷ C3-P0 and R2-D2 taking time off from the battle against Darth Vader and the evil Empire. These are just two of the latest in a long line of science fiction robots.

Laws for robots

In science fiction, robots are often cruel, unfeeling creatures who try to dominate mankind. R2-D2 and C3-P0 are exceptions. Isaac Asimov, the science fiction writer, has devised laws that would have to be followed if people were ever to invent a truly intelligent robot. The laws are designed to protect humans from robots, and would be programmed into robots when they were made. Law 1 states: a robot may not injure a human being. Law 2: a robot must obey orders, except where such orders conflict with law 1. Law 3: a robot must protect itself, except where such protection would conflict with laws 1 and 2.

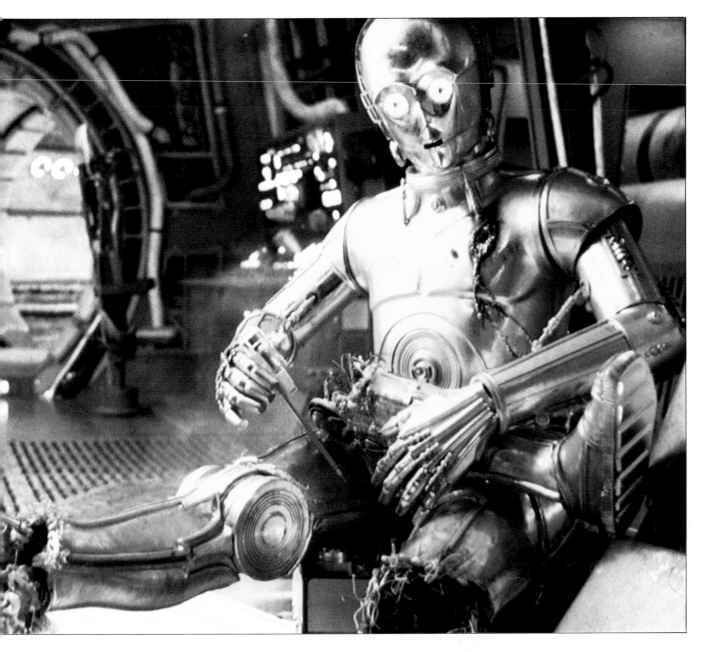

Robots today

Real robots look nothing like people. The only parts of a human body that have been copied are the arm and hand, since most practical jobs are done with the arms. Like a human arm, a robot's arm can swivel, sweep, and move sideways, and bend at the shoulder, elbow and wrist. Usually, they are fitted with a simple gripper that acts like a hand.

Parts of a robot

The instructions that control a robot come from a microprocessor – a kind of miniaturized electronic computer. It contains a few simple instructions, sufficient for the job at hand, and can be reprogrammed with new instructions when the task changes. The robot's "strength" is either provided by fluid under pressure driving pistons inside their cylinders, or by electric motors. Pressure pads in its gripper stop it from squeezing too tightly.

▽ All robots have tiny computers to direct their work. Very advanced robots may have cameras, which operate like human eyes, and microphones which act as ears. Touch is provided by pressure-sensitive pads, power by hydraulic fluids or electricity sent along pipes or cables.

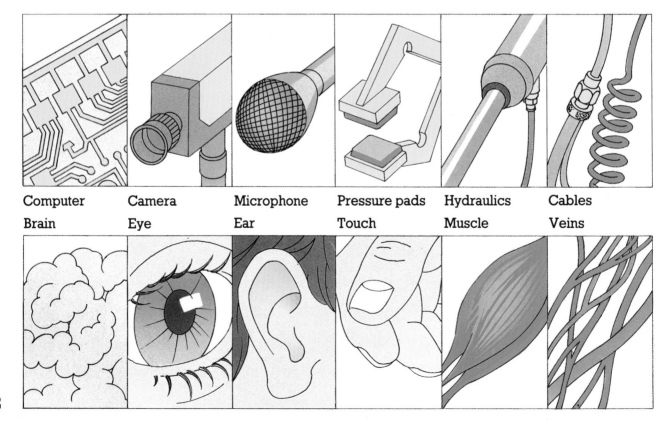

| Computer | Camera | Microphone | Pressure pads | Hydraulics | Cables |
| Brain | Eye | Ear | Touch | Muscle | Veins |

A typical industrial robot looks like this. It is fixed to the ground and the production line moves past it. It can pick things up with a gripper (shown here), a suction pad or even a magnet. The gripper is attached to a part that acts like a wrist. It can bend up and down, side to side and, unlike a human wrist, rotate right around. The "wrist" is carried by the arm, which is mounted onto a central pivot rather like the human shoulder. The whole robot can swivel around on its mountings, driven by hydraulic and electric power.

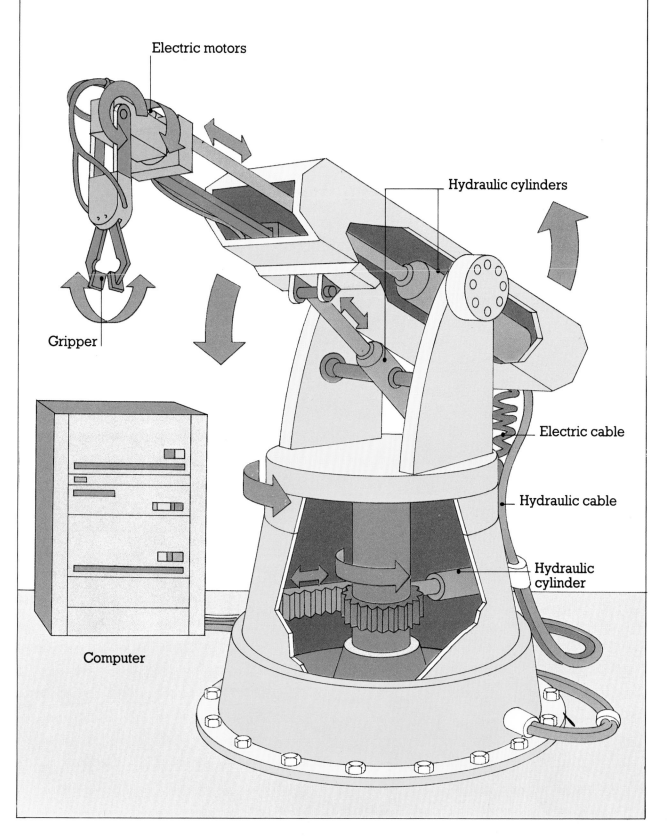

Electric motors

Gripper

Hydraulic cylinders

Electric cable

Hydraulic cable

Hydraulic cylinder

Computer

Programming a robot

The same robot can do many different jobs, unlike, for example, a coffee-making machine, which can do only one. A single robot can be used to assemble, weld and paint the frames of a washing machine. But between each stage, the tools carried by the robot's "hand" have to be changed, and for each job its "memory" must be reprogrammed with fresh instructions.

$\triangleright$ Robots can be instructed using a remote control unit. Just as with other methods of instruction, the robot will store the sequence of movements in its memory.

Instructing a robot

There are two ways of telling a robot what to do. The simplest method is to guide the machine through all the moves it has to make. The robot's computer stores these movements in its memory and the robot can repeat them in exactly the same way every time. The alternative is to use a keyboard to punch detailed instructions into the robot's memory. Unlike humans, a robot never loses concentration. Its work is just as good at the end of the day as at the beginning.

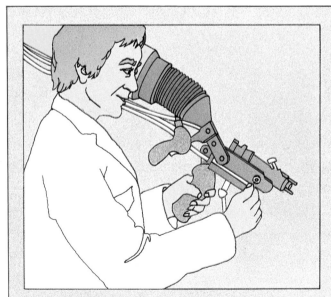

Teaching by doing: to teach a robot how to paint a chair, the operator first attaches handles and a tool – in this case a spray gun – to the robot arm.

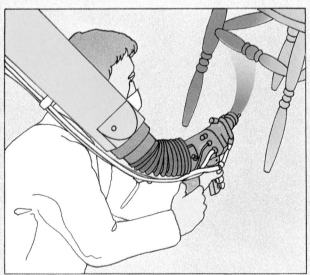

Then he paints the chair himself, moving the arm back and forth. The robot's memory learns the movements and repeats them as required.

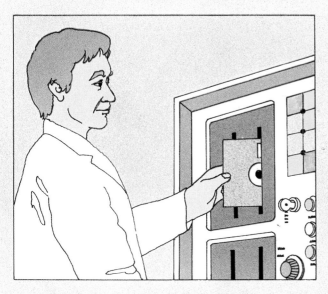

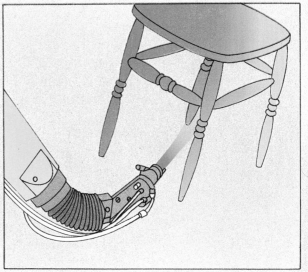

The robot's computer can store the sequence of movements in its memory. The instructions can also be held on a floppy disk, to be slotted into the computer when needed.

The robot will follow the movements in its memory, or those punched in via the keyboard. To change the job, the operator has to put in a different memory disk.

Industrial robots

Robots are useful for repetitive jobs that do not require human judgment. In factories, they are used for welding pieces of metal together, particularly car bodies, and for painting, or for picking things up and loading them onto the production line. Robots never tire of these jobs, so the quality does not vary.

Robot superworkers

For jobs like these, robots have real advantages. When a new model of a car is being introduced, the same production line can be used, with the robots reprogrammed. This is much easier and cheaper than building a new line. Robots are also fast. General Electric in the United States uses robots to assemble 320 compressors an hour, 24 hours a day – the same output as ten workers could produce. At Chrysler's car production plant in Detroit, 50 robots replaced 200 welders – and increased the output.

▽ Robots are ideal to keep pace with a busy production line. The robots do this repetitive work faster and more efficiently than human beings can.

△ The Robogate system, at the Fiat car plant in Italy, employs robots that move the car bodies around the factory. The robots follow tracks laid into the factory floor.

◁ On the Austin-Metro production line, cars are welded by robots. It takes eight minutes to weld each one, and a new car body comes off the line every 42 seconds – a production rate that would be impossible without robots.

17

Robots in transportation

Robots may not be as clever or as versatile as human beings, but they seldom make mistakes. So there are advantages in using robots to fly planes, to drive trains, even perhaps, one day, to drive cars. Already aircraft are sometimes flown by robots known as automatic pilots, especially for routine flying. But at takeoff and landing the pilot takes over, ready to deal with any unforseen circumstances that may arise – robots cannot deal with the unexpected.

Robot teachers

One of the most useful applications of robots in transportation is in flight simulation. This safely trains pilots, without their leaving the ground. The simulator has a cockpit which moves and tilts, and has a full set of controls. Computers project runway images on the cockpit "windows," and the overall effect is so realistic that some people experience flight sickness!

▽ Simulators can teach ship captains as well as pilots. The Cassim Ship Simulator is used to train the captains of supertankers how to manage their huge and valuable ships.

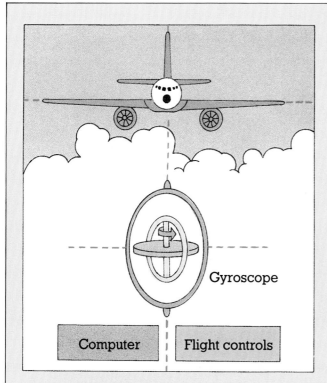

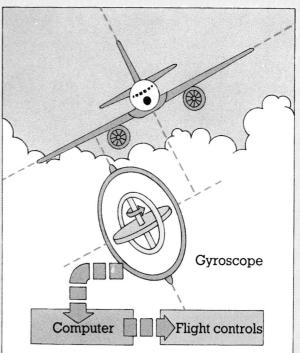

Gyroscope

Computer | Flight controls

Gyroscope

Computer | Flight controls

Civil aircraft today are fitted with automatic pilots – often known familiarly as "George." The system is based on a gyroscope, an instrument that spins constantly and can detect any change of course and altitude. If the plane tilts or alters course, the gyroscope feeds this information into the airliner's on-board computers which automatically adjust the controls, putting the plane back on its correct course.

▷ Lille, in northern France, has a railway system with no drivers. The trains are all controlled from a central computer. The trains stop and start by themselves and the doors open and close automatically. The system came into operation in 1983, and serves 13 stations across the city.

19

Robots in war

Today, many of man's deadliest weapons are robot-controlled. Instead of having to be carefully aimed at the target, like a bullet or an artillery shell, they are fired in the general direction of their targets. They then home in on the heat given off by the target, or on its radar echo, or even its sound. Such "smart" missiles and bombs, as they are called, are almost certain to hit their target after they have been fired.

Map-reading missiles

The most sophisticated of today's robot weapons are Cruise missiles, which fly less than 60 m (197 ft) from the ground, swooping over hills and across valleys. Cruise missiles have computers that store maps of the ground that they have to fly over. Cameras scan the ground and the images are compared with the preprogrammed map. After flying thousands of kilometers, they can identify their target and hit it directly.

▽ Sea-skimming missiles like Sea Skua or Exocet, fly just above the sea, their height controlled by an instrument called an altimeter. They send out a radar beam that bounces off the target, and then home in on the echo.

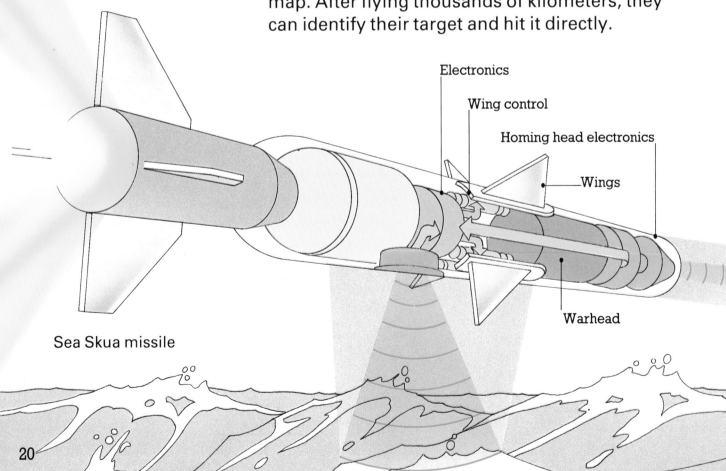

Electronics

Wing control

Homing head electronics

Wings

Warhead

Sea Skua missile

△ Cruise missiles, which can carry either nuclear or ordinary warheads, fly low to avoid radar detection. But they are slow compared with modern aircraft, so, if they are detected (perhaps by radar carried by high-flying aircraft), they can be shot down.

Radar beam

Space robots

The hostile environment of space is ideal for robots, which need no oxygen or complex life-support systems. The Soviet Union's exploration of the Moon, which included landing two Moon "rovers" that wandered about the lunar surface, was all done by remote control robot landers. The United States, however, landed men on the Moon, but explored the planet Mars by sending an unmanned lander. One reason was distance; the Viking lander took eleven months to reach Mars, whereas it takes only three days to reach the Moon.

Robot repairmen

One day soon, robots may be sent into orbit to repair the many satellites used for communications, navigation and weather forecasting. Launched from the space shuttle, the robot spacecraft could carry tools and spares, like a car breakdown service on Earth.

▽ Two Lunokhod moon rovers were landed on the Moon, in 1970 and 1973. Lunokhod 2 traveled 50 km (31 miles) across the surface, sending back pictures. Its power came from solar cells, used to recharge its batteries.

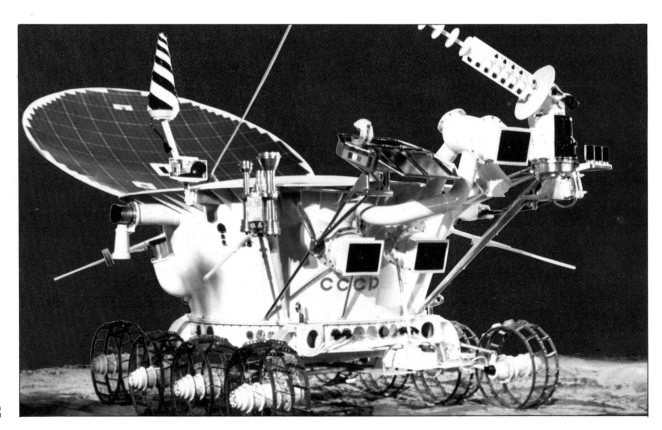

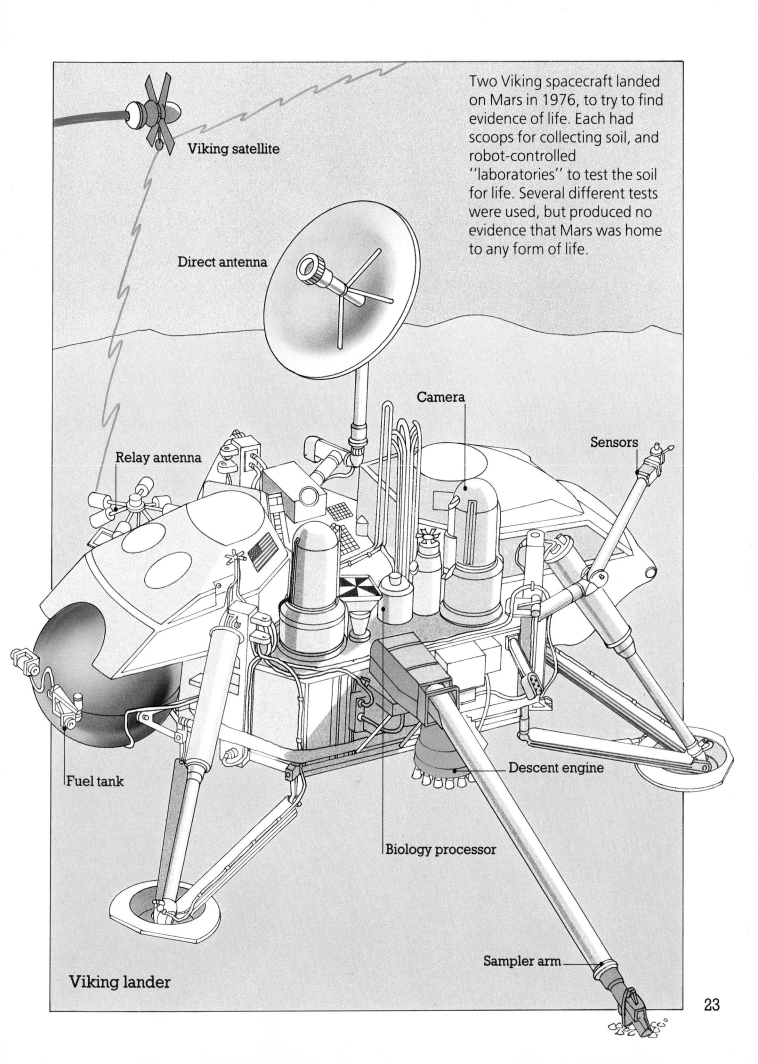

Viking satellite

Two Viking spacecraft landed on Mars in 1976, to try to find evidence of life. Each had scoops for collecting soil, and robot-controlled "laboratories" to test the soil for life. Several different tests were used, but produced no evidence that Mars was home to any form of life.

Direct antenna

Camera

Sensors

Relay antenna

Fuel tank

Descent engine

Biology processor

Sampler arm

Viking lander

23

Remote control

There are many places on Earth almost as dangerous as space: deep in the ocean, for example, or inside the core of a nuclear reactor. But the kind of jobs that have to be done in such places are often not the simple repetitive tasks that robots are best suited to. Such jobs are often done by a form of remote control called *telechirics*. These are machines that are controlled at a distance by man. Control signals are sent along wires, by radio, or through mechanical links to tell the machines, what to do.

Is it a bomb?

One of the best such devices is a bomb detector, "Wheelbarrow," used by the British Army. It trundles over to any suspicious object to examine it with a TV camera. Another good example is the huge "arm" in the space shuttle which is used to launch satellites.

▽ Wheelbarrow is controlled through a cable and equipped with a TV camera and devices for defusing bombs. Should the bomb explode, the controllers are far enough away to avoid injury.

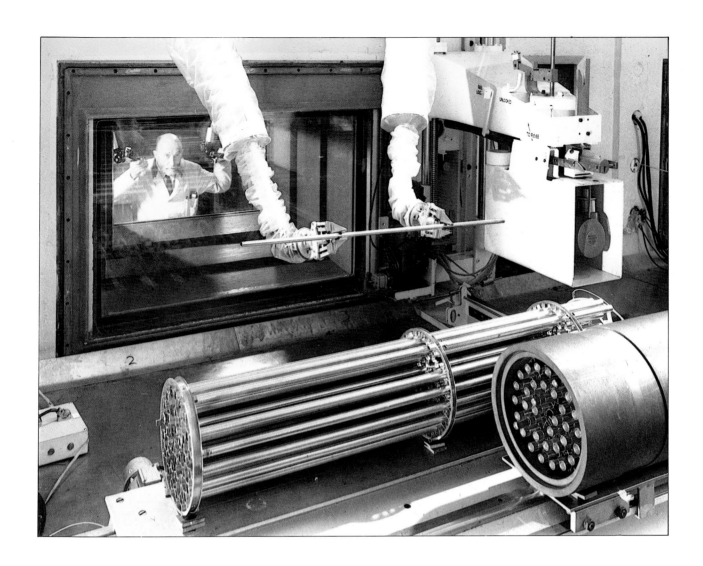

△ Radioactive materials, such as spent fuel from a nuclear power station, are lethal. They are handled from behind thick lead glass, using a device called a "master-slave manipulator."

▷ Working deep under water is difficult and dangerous, so remote control "submersibles" that send pictures back to the surface are often used. But for most underwater jobs, the intelligence of a diver is needed.

Intelligent robots?

The next generation of robots in general use will be able to see. Their eyes will be TV cameras, scanning the scene and sending back pictures to the robot's "brain." This will make robots much more useful. From a jumbled mass of different components, a seeing robot will be able to select the ones it needs, in the right order, and then assemble them into a product. It will identify faulty components and reject them, taking over the task of quality control now done by humans.

▽ Experimental robots developed in Japan have several TV cameras acting as eyes. They identify components and fit them together in the correct alignment. "Second generation" robots of this sort will be much more powerful than today's simple machines.

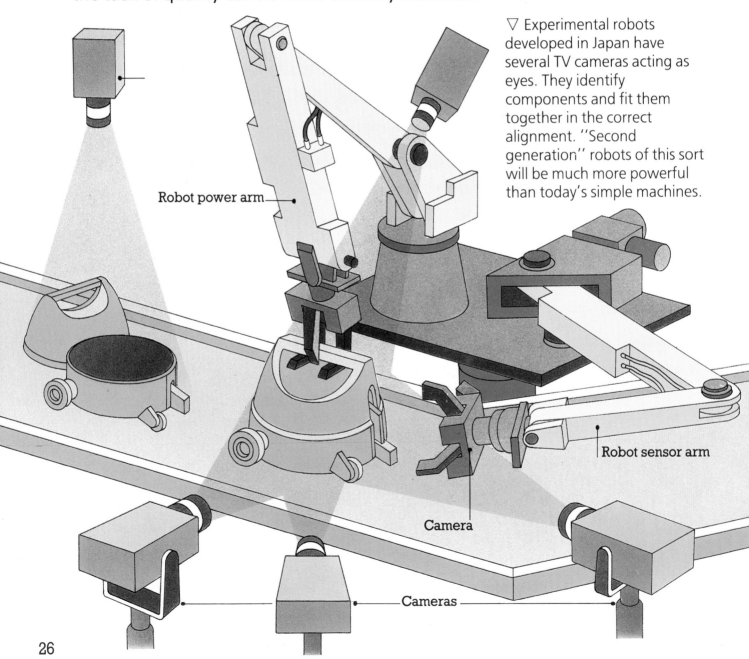

Robot power arm

Robot sensor arm

Camera

Cameras

Thinking machines

The final challenge is to produce robots that can not only do and see, but think as well. Such machines are still a long way in the future, but engineers are already working on the possibility. Thinking robots could do many jobs which are beyond the capacity of today's robots. They could learn from experience and apply logic to solving problems. Already computer programs can diagnose diseases, work out chemical structures and tell farmers why their crops aren't flourishing. Perhaps some time in the next century intelligent robots which run our homes and offices may become a reality.

▽ Satellite repair vehicles of the future will move around space under their own power. When they reach the disabled satellite, they will lock onto it, then go about repairing the satellite, using their own "intelligence." They will carry all the tools they need, and receive instructions from ground stations on Earth.

Glossary

Altimeter	An instrument that measures the height of an aircraft or missile above the ground.
Android	A robot designed to look like a human being.
Automation	The process of producing objects using machines which operate with a minimum of human intervention.
Computer	A machine which uses small electrical currents flowing through circuits to make rapid calculations, to process information and to control operations.
Gyroscope	A wheel rotating within a ring which resists being twisted, making it always point in the same direction.
Hydraulics	The use of a fluid, either liquid or gas, to transmit force by driving a piston inside a cylinder.
Program	Instructions fed into a computer to enable it to perform calculations, control operations and process data. To reprogram a computer is to insert fresh instructions that will make it perform different operations.
Simulator	A system which imitates the behavior of an airplane, ship, tank or weapon and is used to train users cheaply and safely.
Submersible	A vessel which can be submerged in deep water to undertake repair, observation and inspection.
Telechirics	The use of remote-control devices to carry out dangerous work without risk to the operator.

Index

Acknowledgements
The publishers wish to thank the following people who have helped in the preparation of this book:
British Leyland, British Robot Association, Centre Nationale de la Recherche Scientifique, Colne Robotics, Fairey Systems, Institut National de Recherche et de Documentation

Pedagogiques, Unimation, Westinghouse Corporation.

Photographic Credits:
Cover: Tony Stone, *title page:* UKAEA, page 8: Zefa, page 9: Cooper-West, page 10/11: Lucas Films Ltd, page 15: Jim Pickerell (Photri), page 16: Tony Stone, page 17: Fiat; British Leyland, page 18: Marconi, page 19: Comeli,

page 21: AP color photo from the Air Force, page 22: Mat Irvine, page 24: British Army Explosive Ordnance Disposal Team, page 25: UKAEA; Amatek Straza, page 27: NASA (Space Frontiers).